I0440212

Sales: The Best Damn Job in Corporate America

by

Philip A. Keith

Professor of Marketing

and

CEO, Peconic Bay Consulting

© Peconic Bay Consulting, Southampton, NY, 2010

Table of Contents:

Foreword

Hard-hitting. Useful. Motivational. Compact. These are the adjectives I would use to describe the style of this book. Beyond that, my purposes for writing this guide are twofold: one, to quickly uncover if you are cut out for a career in sales and two, if you are, to give you the information and tools that you will need to be successful. It's just that simple.

Some of you may have found this pithy tome on-line or on the shelves of your local bookstore in the "how to" or business section. If so, you were probably looking for a personal resource or self-help guide on the sales profession. If so, you have found it.

Perhaps some of you got this treatise as a give-away at your latest company sales meeting or as a hand-out at the firm's most recent sales training evolution. As such, my experiences dictate that you'll probably either pitch this book right before "happy hour" or put it aside: just another useless piece of pontification from the HR or Training Departments. That would be a mistake. I would submit to you that every sales professional, from greenest rookie to most proficient veteran, will find at least one—if not more—golden nugget of wisdom somewhere in these pages. This is not a boast. It is a promise.

Some of you may have been required to buy this book by one of your business professors as an addition to your assigned readings. If this is the case, please pay special attention to the sections on honesty and integrity. They are my pet causes in business and I'm glad to get a crack at you in the learning stage before you go out and commit some of the stupid and egregious errors that too many business people are making these days.

And here's another promise: If I can get you to read this book just once, you will not throw it away or place it on some dusty bookshelf. I bet if you read this book you will end up sticking it in your briefcase or in the front pocket of your roll-aboard. This guide, you will discover, is also a Road Warrior's Handbook. Once you begin to appreciate the universal truths contained herein this pocket powerhouse will become a constant professional companion. You will—and should—pull it out when you've gone through all the airline magazines in the seat pocket in front of you or when the laptop begins to flash "low battery."

I hope you will use this book as a resource to fall back on when you've gotten off track and nothing seems to be working for you. This happens to everyone in sales at one time or another. My hope is that your copy will become dog-eared from constant use. I also ask that you send me your feedback, suggestions and comments. I'd love to have you share your field experiences with me. If you do, I will include the best of your comments in future editions of this book.

So, here you go: good luck and good selling.

Phil Keith
Southampton, NY
© 2010

Introduction

I firmly believe that true sales ability is in the genes. The best traits of highly successful sales people are characteristics that come pre-programmed. I have seen it countless times: great instructors and well-constructed syllabi can train willing candidates to be good sales people but the greatest sales people have a hereditary head-start. True sales talent is innate. Those who have the "sales gift" smile more readily, shake hands more firmly, look you in the eye every time and palpably radiate enthusiasm for the game. They are better speakers, better listeners, and intuitive problem solvers. They always see lemonade where others only see a bin full of lemons.

Does this mean that those born without these traits cannot be great sales people? No, it doesn't. I have also known some truly excellent and highly successful sales people who were not blessed with in-born selling skills. The difference between these professionals and their natural counterparts is that they invariably had to work harder, struggle longer, fight failure more often and swim upstream further to achieve success in sales. Some of these folks have ended up both wealthy and happy. Many, however, have been miserable for most of their careers even though they ended up at the top of their respective heaps.

Thousands of capable, talented business people commence careers in sales only to crash and burn: some sooner, some later. It happens, in part, because of our skewed cultural business perspective. Too often we place people in sales positions that have absolutely no business being there. The job of "sales rep" is often the entry level position in most industries. If you are not a Wharton MBA or a Strategic Marketing Specialist from Harvard, you are probably going to be tossed into the Darwinian General Sales Pit. Only the fittest survive that experience. If you do only then are you deemed good enough to begin the long, slow climb up the corporate ladder. It's the exact opposite of what should be occurring.

Here's what I mean: sales is every company's life's blood. If your firm's products and services are not in front of qualified buyers who are ready, willing and able to make positive purchasing decisions in your favor then your company is doomed to fail. This is the "front line," people! Only your very best warriors should be on that front line.

Back in the day, right out of college, I was shipped off to Navy Flight School to become a pilot. (My generation had to worry about The Draft and Vietnam before grad school or a career.) After a grueling year of initial flight training those of us who hadn't washed out could look forward to some choice of which aircraft we wanted to ultimately fly (subject to "the needs of the service," of course). The hot-shots and gung-ho warriors picked the high-powered supersonic jet fighters. The solid, steady aviators (who would later become airline pilots) got second choice, mostly the fixed-wing patrol, recon or transport aircraft. The candidates close to the bottom of the class got what was left over, which was usually helicopters. That always struck me as strange: from a pilot's standpoint flying "helos" was far more challenging, physically and mentally, than stick-and-rudder rockets or slow, lumbering cargo-masters. I also knew that if I ended up in trouble (often) and flopped my jet in the drink (I did that once) it would be a helo pilot who would be called to swoop in and pluck my sorry butt out of the water (thank God he did).

Here's where I'm going with this analogy: we tend to do the same thing to young people who want to break into business careers. Unless they are fresh out of Sloan "B" School they are going to be helo pilots. They will be thrown into the middle of huge trading rooms or handed a sample bag and told to go out and sell something. Sink or swim. Fly or die.

If you are about to embark on a career in sales, I'm going to do you a favor, right now, right up front. I'm going to show you how you can determine if selling is for you. And as I have said, not everyone is cut out to be in sales. The sooner you understand this Immutable fact of life the quicker you will be able to move on to whatever it is that you are really meant to do in business. This critical determination will involve a quick test and a little honest soul-searching. If you don't get through my sales gates the price you paid for this book and/or the cost of the time you spent within its pages can be measured against the hundreds of days, maybe years, of pain, agony and frustration you have saved yourself. If you do pass through my gauntlet you can move on to Phase Two: learning what it takes to master the skills you already possess. Ready? Turn the page...

CHAPTER 1: SALES REPRESENTATIVE --THE BEST DAMN JOB IN CORPORATE AMERICA

A company can have the best product or service since the proverbial loaf of sliced bread but if nobody in the company can sell, it'll be stale bread, indeed. Sales is the most important job in the organization. The best designers, production managers, human resource specialists, marketing experts, CIO's, CFO's and CEO's should get down on their knees every morning and pray that they have the best salespeople out in the field. Wouldn't it be grand to have that kind of job—where even the CEO worships at your feet? You bet it would!

In any sales-driven organization the top sales people are the most highly compensated employees. The best sales people have bigger mortgages, faster cars and larger yachts. They also tend to have more friends, go more places, give more to charities and have the most time off. They come and go as they please and get more done with less stress. "How can I get a job like that," you ask?

The best-of-the-best salespeople have worked diligently to get where they are but I find that they have not only worked hard: they have also worked smart. Being smart they first had to work to figure out if they were even cut out to do what they do. So, let's start with an acid test. Read the following questions and answer them quickly and honestly. Nobody but *you* is going to grade or see the test results so, for once, there is no pressure to perform or try and fool anyone—and the last person you want to fool with this test is yourself. Sit back in whatever for you is a quiet, peaceful environment, turn off the cell phone, and take a few minutes to mark an answer to each of the following twenty questions. After you take the test I will help you interpret your answers and show you what it all means. Circle how you feel about each question using a zero-to-five scale with "0" meaning "I completely disagree" and "5" meaning "I am in total, absolute agreement." The numbers 1-2-3 and 4 are shaded versions of your feelings one way or the other.

#1: I am creative and regularly come up with new ideas on how to do things differently.

0-1-2-3-4-5

#2: I like being pressured, especially if it means coming up with new solutions to difficult challenges.

0-1-2-3-4-5

#3: In a difficult situation I typically take the lead as opposed to waiting to see what happens.

0-1-2-3-4-5

#4: I thrive on new learning opportunities and I am constantly seeking information to help me better myself.

0-1-2-3-4-5

#5: I am a risk taker.

0-1-2-3-4-5

#6: Tough competition makes me a better player.

0-1-2-3-4-5

#7: I wake up every day renewed, re-energized and ready to go to work.

0-1-2-3-4-5

#8: I believe in a good balance between my work and my personal life.

0-1-2-3-4-5

#9: My family and friends all agree that I have what it takes.

0-1-2-3-4-5

#10: I would rather lead the discussion than take part in it even if I don't know much about the subject at hand.

0-1-2-3-4-5

#11: Given a choice between doing it right and getting it done I'll choose getting it right.

0-1-2-3-4-5

#12: If I don't know the answer to a tough question I'll find out before committing myself.

0-1-2-3-4-5

#13: What lights my fire is, win lose or draw, just being in the game.

0-1-2-3-4-5

#14: I believe that success is measured by personal satisfaction versus accumulated wealth.

0-1-2-3-4-5

#15: I'd rather have my own business than be the most successful person in somebody else's company.

0-1-2-3-4-5

#16: There is nothing more important to me, in business, than being recognized for my achievements.

0-1-2-3-4-5

#17: Teamwork is not as important to me as my own individual success.

0-1-2-3-4-5

#18: Flexibility is more important than sticking to the plan.

0-1-2-3-4-5

#19: Personality is more important than knowledge.

0-1-2-3-4-5

#20: I have an absolute belief that I was somehow meant to be professionally involved in sales.

0-1-2-3-4-5

Now, total up your points: twenty questions and a possible five points per question gets a max of 100 points. If your total is 50 points or less you do not want a career in sales. Period. You don't have the stamina, interest or motivation for a career in selling. Stop reading this book right now and give it away to someone else who might be able to use it. You are, I am sure, a perfectly wonderful person with lots of potential but that potential is not geared toward a career in sales. If you ignore this advice you have a long road ahead. You may ultimately navigate that road successfully but it will be, I promise you, a trip full of potholes, speed bumps and land mines. Please take my advice and do something else. You will be much happier and someday you will thank me.

If you scored between 51 and 79 points you have some sales potential. I will let you be the judge as to what to do with this knowledge but if it were my future on the line, with a score in this range; I'd seriously be considering other options—perhaps marketing. You will have a slightly enhanced sales profile if you gave yourself 4's or 5's on Questions 3, 6, 11, 13 and 20, so go back and take a look.

If you scored 80 to 90 you've got excellent sales potential. If you scored 91 or above you are one of the sales "naturals" I discussed in the Introduction. What are you waiting for! Go sell something!

Let me explain a little about the questions—unless, of course, you scored 50 or below because if you did you don't give a damn and you've already stop reading, correct?

QUESTION 1: *"I am creative and regularly come up with new ideas on how to do things differently."*
A successful sales person has to be creative. Being able to think on one's feet, overcome objections and devise new solutions on-the-fly is often the determining factor between winning and letting your competitor seize the day.

QUESTION 2: *"I like being pressured, especially if it means coming up with new solutions to difficult challenges."*
The competition is always trying to eat your lunch. They will do anything and everything they can to get your customers to tell you, "No!" Being able to dodge competitive bullets and sort out difficult challenges is a key factor in sales success. If you don't like challenges even a bullet-proof vest won't help.

QUESTION 3: *"In a difficult situation I typically take the lead as opposed to waiting to see what happens."*
If you can't wrestle the lead away from your competition time after time you are destined to be left waiting around to see what happens—and it generally won't be a pretty sight.

QUESTION 4: *"I thrive on new learning opportunities and I am constantly seeking information to help me better myself."*
The very best sales people are always seeking to learn more: about their own products, their prospects, their customers and their competitors.

QUESTION 5: *"I am a risk taker."*
If you can't stand risk, don't go into sales. Sales involves risk-taking every single day; plus, most sales positions depend on sales commissions and commissions

(=) risk.

QUESTION 6: *"Tough competition makes me a better player."*
If you don't like competition you shouldn't be in sales. More than this, though, you should thrive on competition and you should believe that competition improves your skills, because it will.

QUESTION 7: *"I wake up every day renewed, re-energized and ready to go to work."*
Every day is a new challenge for great sales people; in fact, there is a saying about this that is very apt: "There's nothing older than yesterday's commissions." You must be open to new challenges every day. You must be able to put yesterday's defeats and even yesterday's victories behind you every morning. Remember this: every day, at dawn, the score is zero-zero and it's a whole new ball game.

QUESTION 8: *"I believe in a good balance between my work and my personal life."*
Balance is essential to your long-term physical and mental health. Focus is critically important to sales success but so is stepping back once in a while. Sales is conflict. Sales is war. You need a good support system to continue to win battle after battle. Take time out for family, friends, recreation and reflection.

QUESTION 9: *"My family and friends all agree that I have what it takes."*
I have found that the top sales people are immediately recognized for what they are by their families and friends. They have a confident air and bear all the hallmarks of success. They make people smile and everyone wants to be associated with them. People will say things about them like, "He/She is really going somewhere."

QUESTION 10: *"I would rather lead the discussion than take part in it even if I don't know much about the subject at hand."*
Great sales talent leads, it never follows. It is a process of taking every prospect from "suspect" to satisfied customer. Great salespeople have to have what the Irish call "the gift of blarney." Blarney is not "BS," by the way. BS is a curse, not

11

a gift. BS always gets discovered, most times on the bottom of the BSer's own shoes. Blarney is not prevarication either; it is the gift of being a great talker. Without blarney sales conversation does not come naturally.

QUESTION 11: *"Given a choice between doing it right and getting it done I'll choose getting it right."*
We still treat salespeople stereotypically in our culture. Either they are viewed as pathetic Willy Loman types or sales cowboys: "all hat and no cattle." We don't tell our families and friends, "When my kids grow up I hope they go into sales!" But somehow the very best in the sales profession have, in my experience, been the most principled, the most honest, and the most empathetic business professionals I have ever met. They "get it" and doing it right is more important than simply getting it done.

QUESTION 12: *"If I don't know the answer to a tough question I'll find the answer before committing myself."*
Another popular misconception about sales people is that they will tell you anything to get the sale, especially if it's what you want to hear. It's the old "used car salesman" syndrome. There are certainly sales people that still deserving the stereotype but they are the lazy and dishonest members of our profession. The best salespeople, on the other hand, work hard for their customers and part of doing that is making sure they get honest answers to all of their questions. Sometimes that means admitting they don't know the answer to a question. Now, that takes courage!

QUESTION 13: *"What lights my fire is, win lose or draw, just being in the game."*
The best sales people have a love for the game, a desire to be in the arena. Being constantly subjected to the challenges of successful selling is what gets the juices flowing for these people every day. If you dread the thought of taking the ball and running with it you should not be in sales.

QUESTION 14: *"I believe that success is measured by personal satisfaction versus accumulated wealth."*
The best salespeople I know generally have a very high level of measurable success and feelings of immense personal satisfaction for how they arrived at where they are. My unscientific observations of those who think that money is

more important than personal satisfaction are (a) they are generally self centered jerks and (b) they are miserable people.

QUESTION 15: *"I'd rather have my own business than be the most successful person in somebody else's company."*
Even if you work within a very large sales force in a very big Fortune 500 company you are still, by and large, responsible for your own success or failure. As a sales professional in a business, big or small, you are a business within a business; the business of YOU! If you embrace and appreciate the entrepreneurial nature of sales you are well on your way to becoming successful at selling.

QUESTION 16: *"There is nothing more important to me, in business, than being recognized for my achievements."*
Great sales people have to have a streak of vanity. There are more daily challenges than successes so when they win they like to be recognized for what they have achieved. Recognition keeps them sharp, motivated, satisfied and well paid. A little vanity, in this case, is a good thing.

QUESTION 17: *"Teamwork is not as important to me as my own individual success."*
This question is not meant to demean or belittle the importance of teamwork. Team selling and being an effective member of a sales team can be very important attributes to a good sales organization. Good sales people understand the value of being team players. BUT! Great sales people also know that when the chips are down the one person who is going to be most responsible for their success or failure is the one that they will see in the bathroom mirror tomorrow morning.

QUESTION 18: *"Flexibility is more important than sticking to the plan."*
Successful selling is a constantly moving target. Situations and customer needs can change, prices can change, and competitors can turn on a dime. To be truly successful in sales you must have a plan but any good plan must have an element of flexibility built into it. If you don't like change don't get into the sales profession!

QUESTION 19: *"Personality is more important than knowledge."*
The smartest sales people understand clearly that product and customer knowledge are two critical keys to success but if you can't inject some personality into the sales situation it's going to be a much tougher road to travel. The world's best sales people are those whose yearbook pictures were captioned with phrases like: "Lights up the room upon entering;" or, "Voted Best Personality."

QUESTION 20: *"I have an absolute belief that I was somehow meant to be professionally involved in sales."*
If there's one question on this test that is more important than any other question it is this one. If you didn't give yourself at least a 4 or even better a 5, it's doubtful you should embark on a sales career.

If you passed my little test, congratulations: you have sales potential. Now read on and learn how to be the best damn salesperson you can possibly be.

CHAPTER 2: THE MOST COMMON CHARACTERISTICS OF SUCCESSFUL SALES PEOPLE:

There is no one-size-fits-all, best of the best, tried-and-true selling style or method. If that were the case, sales training would be a breeze and selling would be a picnic and we know neither of those things is true. But I also know this: as I look back on the most successful sales people I have known, there are a common set of characteristics they all share, no matter their individual selling styles or personalities. Here they are:

1. They have a LOVE FOR THE GAME: I can talk with you for five minutes and tell if you are meant to be in sales—or not. If it's that obvious to me, a perfect stranger, it sure as hell ought to be obvious to you. Those who are meant to be in sales have a glint in the eyes, a quiet determination about them and a love for the game that will be apparent. They will be tigers who have a fire-in-the-belly type determination to overcome all obstacles that may be placed in their paths. They have an air of "I will not be defeated" about them. Even if they have never been in sales, I can tell if they will be successful in sales. Why? Because they will be fidgety, edgy and anxious to get going, to learn more about this exciting aspect of business and I will see that they can be taught the skills they will need. They will have no fear of rejection. Most of all, they will have an over-riding absolute confidence about them that they will succeed in sales and when asked if this is where they want to be they will not hesitate to say "Yes!"

2. They have HONESTY: One of the best rewards for telling the truth is

15

that you never have to remember what you said. If you've spoken the truth from the beginning you never have to be worry about being caught in a lie. Sometimes telling the truth isn't easy, pleasant or especially productive. Your customer will not want to hear that the shipment they are counting on has been delayed or that you can't meet the deadline you promised because of some tornado in Kansas. Sometimes your competitors will be able to take advantage of you by telling their own lies. They may get business away from you but I promise it'll only be temporary. I have yet to see an honest salesperson lose an account for telling the truth—maybe they lose some business in the short run, as customers have to adjust to realities, but they never lose in the long run. In contrast, I have seen a bazillion times when customers have been lost for good and reputations destroyed through lies. Buyers always come back to sellers who have been honest with them. Truth-telling makes you feel good at the end of the day and on that basis alone it carries its own reward. Telling the truth is a powerful sales advantage in and of itself.

3. They have INTEGRITY: and integrity is different than honesty, although they both go hand-in-hand. If you have integrity you are solid: you can be relied upon. Buyers can smell integrity and they love to be associated with it because it rubs off and makes them look good, too. If you have integrity you will have the fairest pricing structures. Customers will know they can't get any better deal than that which they can get from you. If you have integrity you are believable and buyers buy from those they can believe in. Practice integrity. Live Integrity. If you do your sales will know no limits.

4. They have DISCIPLINE: The best salespeople have discipline; that is to say, they have a routine. Notice I did not say they are "regimented." That's not the kind of discipline we are talking about. Disciplined sales people have a work ethic and a methodology that has common threads. Take some of the following strands and weave them into your own winning sales discipline:

    a: Recognize your own biorhythms: For example, I work best

between the hours of 6 AM and 9 AM. When I'm not on the road, I am at my desk at 6 AM, coffee mug in hand. This is the most productive time of my day. It is when I am at my best and most alert. It's also a quiet period in my own time zone, before the phone starts ringing. If you're not an early riser, that's OK. Maybe you work best from 9 AM to noon, or noon to 3 PM. Get to know what works best for you and use this time to conduct the tasks that are essential to your selling preparation: strategy, planning, paperwork.

   b: Schedule your calling time: Salespeople don't make sales unless they are in front of prospects and buyers in person, by phone, or via web presence. Determine when you are going to make your calls and stick to a schedule. Time your calls to your peak performance times, too, if you can.

   c: Plan your work and work your plan: Whatever your plan is (much more on this to follow), stick to it: not slavishly but doggedly. If you've done your homework properly you've made a good plan. There will always be distractions, emergencies, even unanticipated windfalls that will try and distract you from your plan. As soon as they are dealt with, get back to the plan.

   d: Schedule down-time: This is office time, off the road time, admin time. This is where you catch up on all the e-mail, answer your correspondence, send out the info packets, return non-urgent calls, and revise your plans. Schedule this time! If you don't, the necessary but onerous "administrivia" will eventually overwhelm you.

5. They have PERSISTENCE: As the saying goes, "nothing beats persistence." The best sales people have persistence in abundance. Persistence is not an attitude of "I'm never taking no for an answer." It is more of an attitude of "I will never be defeated." Persistent salespeople will always find a way to get the job done. Sometimes this can mean going around an obstacle rather than trying to smash through it. Persistence can sometimes mean recognizing you are in an impossible situation and that it's time to move on to the next opportunity.

6. They have BASIC ORGANIZATION: Every good salesperson that I know is very organized. Some are equipped with the latest high-tech gadgets and

some are not. It doesn't really matter as long as you have a systematic approach to sales and one that is comfortable for you. Certainly there is an incredible arsenal of high-tech tools available today: Blackberry's, the Internet, multi-function cell phones, PDA's, contact management software (such as ACT! and Goldmine). I suggest you try some of these tools for yourself to see which one or ones suit you best; however, high-tech is not always the ultimate approach. I have seen people absolutely get lost in the lure of technology and forget some of the basics--like person-to-person contact.

I, myself, am a middle-of-the-road-type: I use a contact manager, a laptop, the Internet and a pretty sophisticated cell phone. But I still write notes by hand and use long-hand Blueprints (more on these later) to scope out my best prospects and plot strategy. I still write notes to myself on a daily basis and try to take the best of these notes and type them into my electronic backup system.

Whatever methodology you use the key is this: you must have some way of organizing your appointments, tracking your contacts and deploying your sales strategy. You must have (at a minimum) an appointment book (paper-based or electronic), a file of some sort for each prospect and client, a convenient method to work every contact you intend to pursue, and a comprehensive contact list. My contact list resides on my laptop, a copy exists on my cell phone and I keep a paper printout of the same in my briefcase.

Basic organization can be a book in and of itself, and maybe when this book is done I'll start on that one, but for now you must, *must*, develop an organizational methodology and deploy it. Keep refining it as you go. Stick with what works and toss out what doesn't until you get to the point where you can teach basic organization to sales trainees. Keep watching and looking at the organizational systems used by your own company's best salespeople and spy on the competition, too!

7. They have PRODUCT KNOWLEDGE: The very best salespeople know their products and product lines as well as they know their own names and dates of birth. I once had the rare privilege of working with a man who was, hands-down, absolutely one of the very best sales people I ever ran across, and he was a toilet paper salesman. Toilet paper! This was at the

old and long since gone Crown-Zellerbach Paper Co. in San Francisco. I was the rookie marketing analyst and he was the senior sales rep and the Dean of his era of old-fashioned, hard-working, bag-carrying salesmen. Henry had been at it for more than fifty years and he was just as enthusiastic for the business in his late seventies as he had been in his early twenties. He made it very clear to me that one of his secrets to success was that he knew more about toilet paper than any other bum-wad sales rep in America. He didn't sell boxes of toilet tissue: he sold entire box*cars* of toilet tissue.

With his deep knowledge of single, double and triple plies; colors and dyes; and what his customers said they needed and wanted Henry was even able to influence product development. It was Henry, in fact, who came up with one of the most profitable toilet tissue products in history. It was also the slickest innovation in toilet paper sales in the last hundred years. The product had a devilishly clever name and I bet you've run across it more than once. It was called "No-Waste." This aggravating and annoying personal hygiene product was packed into small metal dispensers and pulled out in single sheets the size of a piece of Kraft sliced cheese. Henry sold this product in staggering quantities to the large industrial companies that had hundreds or thousands of employees. He told them if would save them tons of money over the rolled-type tissues that people tended to use in very wasteful quantities; ergo, the new product name of "No-Waste." The buyers at these big companies loved it. They envisioned their employees (at Henry's suggestion) using a sheet at a time instead of unraveling huge quantities of the more expensive tissue. Well, of course, the employees hated it. In protest they tended to empty the dispensers at a single sitting. But here's the best part: Henry knew the workers would hate it. He knew that they would grab entire catcher's mitt sized wads of "No-Waste," and, well, waste it! Henry knew his customers and he knew his customer's consumers. He had happy customers who were blithely sold on a concept and angry users who ended up wasting more tissue than they ever had before with the old rolls of toilet paper. It was brilliant. It became the company's best-selling paper product and it made Henry very rich. The lesson: even toilet paper can teach us lessons such as "know your customer and know your product".

8. They know that EVERYTHING OLD IS NEW AGAIN: The Chinese general Sun-Tzu wrote a treatise called "The Art of War" over two thousand years ago. Incredibly, his basic principles are still being taught today at our nation's military academies and at the various war colleges. I first ran into the Old General when I was a student at the Naval War College. Sun-Tzu's entire premise is that successful warfare consists of a small number of basics that are over-arching and rock solid. An author with a lot of experience in the corporate world by the name of Gary Gagliardi has written a book for salespeople that adapt Sun-Tzu's principles to the daily battles we face in the sales world. The book is called: "The Art of War for the Sales Warrior: Sun-Tzu's Strategy for Salespeople." I highly recommend you read this book--after mine of course--but in the interim here's the gist of what you will discover: good salespeople are innovative, to be sure, but they don't re-invent the wheel every day.

9. They NEVER STOP LEARNING: Great salespeople are also students of the profession. They will seek out books like this one and Mr. Gagliardi's plus they will eagerly attend sales training evolutions, sign up for sales improvement seminars, wander trade shows for new ideas and participate in on-line seminars on sales training and improvement. They know they don't know it all and they are always eager to learn more.

CHAPTER 3: THE ONLY HARD AND FAST RULES FOR SALES

Sales is a profession that is entrepreneurial, individualistic and fluid. As we have said several times, there is no "one-best-way" to sell. There are, however, at least four rock-solid, hard-and-fast Rules for Selling. You need to understand and appreciate these rules if you are going to be successful in sales.

RULE NUMBER 1: THE 80/20 RULE: No matter what you sell, where you sell or to whom you sell, the 80/20 Rule is the fundamental rule of selling. We don't know exactly why it works but it does. Remember "E=MC2" from your incomprehensible physics book? No-one, not even Einstein, understands just exactly why that formula works either, but it does. The 80/20 Rule is just like that but, mercifully, it's easier to explain. Here it is: "You will get 80% of your sales from 20% of your customers."
Here are some examples:

If you have ten clients and you sell $1 million in product, $800,000 of those sales dollars will come from two of your clients.

If you have 100 clients and sell $500,000 worth of your product, 20 of your clients will have given you sales orders for $400,000.

But there's more: the 80/20 Rule has a gazillion important corollaries:

80% of your new clients will come from 20% of your prospects.
80% of your service calls will come from 20% of your customers.
80% of your complaints will come from 20% of your customers.
80% of your referrals will come from 20% of your customers.
...and so on .

Here's the lesson of this sermon: the 80/20 Rule will unfailingly tell you how to organize yourself for the maximum potential for success. If you spend 80% of your time on the 20% who are your best customers this is where you will get your biggest and best orders.

On a practical basis, this tells me that if I'm working a typical five-day week, I am going to spend four days (80%) interacting with my best customers and one day a week (20%) prospecting for new ones. Or, if I'm just starting out in sales and have few or no customers, I am going to be spending four days a week banging hard to get customers and one day a week doing the organizing, planning, strategizing, sales administration, professional development and office work I need to do to keep up and keep current.

RULE NUMBER TWO: The "I Never Need to Lose" Rule: When I conduct sales training seminars I start the session on "Competition" by telling my audience, "Ladies and gentlemen: you never need to lose a sale." I get many skeptical looks, so what do I mean by this audacious statement? Is it really possible that we can beat the competition every single time? Of course not: sometimes you win, sometimes you lose. The key word in my statement is "need." No-one needs to lose whether it's a sale, a ballgame or a good friend. Let me turn the statement around a bit: sometimes it's important to choose to lose. Confused? Here's the message: learn to recognize when it's time to walk away. Sometimes this concept is just as critical as skillful cold calling, prospecting or closing. Losing is negative: it affects the psyche. Losing is "bad" and when we lose sales we start a negative cycle that can spiral from blaming ourselves or others to questioning our very involvement in the profession. If you can master the trick of deciding to win when you know you can win and choose to walk away when you know you can't, you'll never lose. Here's how I learned this lesson in dramatic fashion. Thank goodness it was early in my sales career:

When I first got into sales I had no experience. At the time, I was working for a high-tech educational software company in San Diego. The task was to sell a then revolutionary new CD-ROM based curriculum to public and private schools. The software could cost tens of thousands of dollars for a site license plus the cost of the computers required to run the programs. It was tough because school budgets were tight and the competition for instructional dollars was intense.

I was pitching my product like crazy in this one particular suburban school district in Riverside County, California. If I could get the deal it was a half-million in revenue and it would certainly make my year. I was determined to win, but I was up against a notoriously competitive saleswoman with a pretty good product and many more years of selling experience than I had at that time. I tried to do everything right: I demonstrated my product, got teacher acceptance, met with the Superintendent, brought in my curriculum experts and got to know everyone I needed to know. I smiled, joked and took many people to lunch or dinner (that was still acceptable practice in those days—not so much anymore).
The Superintendent liked my determination and commitment, and said so. He also favored my product over my competitor's but he called me into his office one day and sat me down to lower the boom. In short, he said, simply, "Nice try. 'A' for effort, but you are not going to get this business."

I was stunned, speechless. Dreams of my new sports car faded before my eyes. "Why?" I whined pitifully.

"Because," the Superintendent responded sympathetically, "this deal was wired for your competitor from Day One. The Chairman of the School Board plays golf every Saturday with his old college roommate who happens to be the Chairman of your competitor's company. You may not like that, but its reality."

I now understood clearly that I was the shill in this process and my attention to the District's needs was an excellent counter-balance to any charge from outsiders that the Board had not looked at other viable alternatives.

As I pondered my next move, like maybe getting rip roaring drunk, the Superintendent went on to say, "But, you know, I've been wondering for weeks now why you've been putting so much effort into our situation when my buddy [the Superintendent in a neighboring school district]

23

needs exactly what you've got, he has the money to buy it right now and he hasn't seen your competition."

That revelation hit me like a ton of DVD's. The hard drive (my pea brain!) was finally warmed up and the lights were coming on. From that moment forward I made up my mind that I would never lose again. I chose to pull out of the competition where I was beating my head against the wall for nothing and I got my fanny down the road to the school district next door. Six weeks later I closed a deal three times bigger.

RULE NUMBER THREE: "You only get one chance to make a first impression:" If your first contact with a prospect is full of promises you cannot keep, you will forever be known to that prospect as someone who cannot deliver. If your first meeting is full of un-truths strewn across the competitive landscape, you will forever be perceived as a liar, no matter how many mea culpas you may cough up.

This lesson was drilled into me, as were so many of the great lessons in my life, by my Navy experiences. We had an axiom in the Navy, and it went like this: If you do something well, you get an "attaboy" (or, today, I suppose, also "attagirls"). If you do something wrong—boy or girl—you get an "awshit." The overall formula for success is, roughly, "One thousand attaboys equals one awshit." The same is true in the sales profession.

If, on the other hand, your first impression is one of honesty, sincerity, eagerness, and a desire to understand the prospect and the prospect's needs, you will forever be looked at as someone who cares, and that is the position you want to be in.

RULE NUMBER FOUR: "The Whoever Speaks Next Loses Rule:" Selling is a constant process and much of the time we are selling we are talking or demonstrating. At some point, however, you just have to stop—and listen. It is sometimes very hard to figure out: when, exactly, have you said enough? It's even more nerve-wracking to stay quiet and wait for your prospect's reactions. This is when the "Whoever Speaks Next Loses" Rule comes into play.

What does it mean? It's a simple sales strategy but it is one of the hardest to execute. If you think you've done enough or said enough, just stop. The next person who speaks—hopefully your prospect—is the "loser." If your prospect starts talking you know one thing for sure: they're listening to you and you are beginning to break down any resistance they might have to you or your product. If they sit there in stony silence it means you haven't smashed through their barriers and they are not listening to you or buying into your pitch: you lose, and you're going to have to re-start the conversation or give up and slink away.

I have witnessed really good sales people use this rule as an enormously effective trial close or, in some cases, as an actual closing tactic. I have used it myself and I remember one time in particular when I knew I had said everything I should say and needed to say and it was time to shut up and listen. I also knew that this particular buyer was notorious in our industry as a real ball-buster who loved to toy with sales people and rake them over the coals. He had tried it with me before and this time I wasn't going to let him get away with it. So, I simply stopped, folded my hands in my lap and stared at Mr. Big. The two of us sat there in complete silence for what seemed to me to be an eternity. A full minute went by. I was about to panic and open my mouth. I could feel the first little beads of sweat forming under my collar. To pass the time I calmly picked up my appointment book and began flipping through the pages pretending to review my upcoming schedule. Another minute went by. Mr. Big still sat staring at me sternly. Finally, mercifully, he glanced at his watch and sighed. I don't know if he wanted to know what time it was, how long we had been sitting there or if he was worried about his next appointment, but whatever it was I knew I had him. He looked right at me and smiled: "All right, we'll go with it. Write it up and bring it back to me for signature."

As much as good sales people have to know when and how to turn on the tap, they also have to know when to shut it off and wait for the waters to settle.

CHAPTER FOUR: THE BEST SALES TOOLS EVER INVENTED:

Sales, not prostitution, is the world's oldest profession. Just look at Eve: the world's second person and she's already selling Adam on the nutritional value of apples. Selling has been with us since the beginning. Natural selection made us who we are today, mostly through increasing brainpower and the ability to invent tools. Your natural ability to be the "brainiest" in sales will also be augmented by tools. In this chapter we will review the best sales tools that have yet been invented. All of them should be in your kit.

Tool #1: "The Six Questions:" Almost every situation in life can be encircled or dissected by the Six Questions: Who-What-When-Where-Why-How. The same is true in sales and the salespeople who master the Six Questions will thoroughly understand each and every sales situation in which they may find themselves.

WHO is the customer? Is it the prospect you are talking with or is it someone else in the organization? Who is the ultimate user or decision maker? If you are not talking with the decision maker(s) you are wasting your time. If you are not talking with the people who are going to be using whatever it is you're selling you have no understanding of your customer, no internal champion and little likelihood of making the sale. The sooner you understand the "who" the shorter your sales cycle will become.

WHAT does the customer really need? Have you done a complete customer analysis or are you trying to sell what you have to anyone who will listen? If you have a line of products are you pitching the right ones? If your company makes a high-quality line of screen doors and your customer builds submarines, what are you doing there?

WHEN will a purchasing decision be made? If there's no budget available until the next fiscal year are you going to sit on their doorstep or put this prospect aside for a while and go get someone else who has funds available now? Side benefit: if you know when the purchasing decisions are going to be made you can look like a sales forecasting genius to your sales manager. You can also help your company allocate its resources if you know all the "whens." This will help get you that new Porsche faster.

WHERE will the action happen? This could mean where your product or service will be applied or where the decisions are made. You need to know both. Lets' say your company receives a proposal for outdoor clothing for maintenance workers. A successful bid response could be affected by knowing whether the workers are in Alaska or Hawaii—or both. If you're hammering away on the purchasing manager in Atlanta when the final decision is going to be made in Chicago, you're in deep trouble.

WHY is this purchase being made? Not as stupid a question as it sounds. People sometimes make irrational purchases. It's the same thing we do when we're strolling down a supermarket aisle and there's an unbelievable special on macaroni and cheese: "ten cans for ten dollars!" Into the cart they go—and your kids hate macaroni and cheese but at these prices you convince yourself they'll love it. Commercial buyers sometimes do the same thing: they fall in love with goods or services they don't need. Easy sale for you but when they end up getting stuck with too much inventory, who are they going to blame? Right-You! It's also good to know the right reasons why these customers are buying. It will help you craft the best deals and set you up as someone who knows and cares about the client.

HOW is this sale going to happen? You want this deal, but do you truly understand the process by which it will be concluded? Do you know the purchasing policies and procedures for your customers? Do you know how they bid and negotiate? Do you understand how purchase orders work their way through the customer's systems and how long it will take before they land in your greedy little mitts?

The Six Questions: I'm sure you can see that there could be many permutations and combinations to these questions but the point is this: if you're serious about the sale you must ask and understand each of the six questions for each and every customer. If you don't, you're flying blind.

TOOL #2: "The Top 25:" How many targets can you chase effectively? Even the very best sales people can only deal with a finite number. If you're dealing with big-ticket, high-potential, Fortune 500 accounts, maybe you only have a "Top 10." If you're selling mass market widgets that are stocked by every hardware store large and small, maybe you have a "Top 50." The point is this: rifle shooting at specific targets bags more game than blasting away with a shotgun in the dark.

Remember the "80/20 Rule" from Chapter 3? Here is where it really applies. You will get 80% of your business from 20% of your customers: why are you chasing those prospects that are not going to be in that 80%? Why are you spending 80% of your time on the 20% who are yanking you around? Focusing on a "Top 25" list will force you to spend 80% of your time on the 20% who will line your pockets with commission dollars. You spend the other 20% of your time on the rest of your customer list and prospecting for new additions to your contact list.

The "Top 25" should be memorialized each and every month on some sort of spreadsheet. This is also a great way to forecast your business. One way of approaching this is shown in the figure below. Figure 4-A is a very simple listing of your very best customers and prospects. It is NOT a forecast. It's just a list to remind you, every day and in every way, where your bread is going to be buttered over the next week, month, quarter, or whatever sales cycle you value most. These are the people with whom you will spend 80% of your time. This list is your sales bible, your daily mantra. Next to each listing is the next activity/project/milestone you should be achieving with each particular client or prospect. This list is nothing more than a daily reality check. It can easily fold into your forecast or sales report (more below) and this list should be carried by you at all times and go under your pillow each night. Some people keep it on a word-processor; some keep it on their PDA's. It doesn't matter. You do what's best for you.

How does someone get on the "Top 25" list? Easy! They're your very best customers and the prospects that you expect will do the most business with you during the next sales cycle.

How does someone drop off the "Top 25"?" Also easy. Their needs are fulfilled for the next sales cycle (and you'll pick them up again when it's right). They have had an event occur that means they no longer deserve your time or energy (merger, acquisition, disaster, bankruptcy, etc.); or, (best of all scenarios) you've found someone bigger and better to put in your "Top 25."

FIGURE 4-A
"TOP 25" List (1)

(7) Rank	(2) Name	(3) Prospect Customer "P" or "C"	(4) Location of Critical Info	(5) Goal	(6) Next Step	CF (8)
1	Example 1	P	PDA	Close on Example Bid	Get Mr. BIG a plan letter	60%
2	Example 2	C	Blueprint	Re-order on last sale	Needs pricing by next week!	80%
3	Example 3	P	Sales notes	$xxx by the end of next quarter	Demo the products to evaluation committee	40%
4						
5						
6						
7						
8						
9						
10						
11						
12						
13						
14						
15						
16						
17						
18						
19						
20						
21						
22						
23						
24						
25						

(1) Remember: The primary goal of a Top 10/25/50 list is to keep your hottest targets, most important goals and the most pressing issues up front and in your sights at all times.
(2) Rank by relative importance, most important at the top.
(3) Name of the actual business entity.
(4) Is this a (P) Prospect or (C) Current Customer?
(5) Where is all information located for this prospect or customer?
(6) What is the next ultimate goal for this prospect or customer?
(7) What is the next step required to get you at or closer to the goal?
(8) What is this prospect's or customer's current CONFIDENCE FACTOR?

TOOL # 3: Confidence Factors: One of the great sales mysteries revolves around trying to determine when business is going to be concluded with a given client or prospect. It's certainly something you, as the most interested party, want to try and figure out, but it is often a key component in creating what every sales manager in America wants to see form you: an accurate sales forecast. The trouble is, forecasting is a "black art" and sales forecasting is often approached as a game called "Stump the Manager." Too often, forecasts are driven not by reality but by hopes and dreams; or worse, lies. You tell your sales manager what you think they want to hear so they will get off your back for a while or let you keep your job a little longer. It doesn't have to be this way.

Have you ever heard a conversation that went something like this? I'll bet you have!

Sales Manager: "Hey, when's that XYZ deal going to close? We need the business!"

Sales Rep: "Boss! It's in the bag! Any day now!"

Sales Manager: "That's great! What's your confidence level for that prediction?"

Sales Rep: "Done deal. Ninety percent...No problem!"

Sales Manager: "Really? So...what does 90% mean?"

Sales Rep: "Er...Ah...Well, like I said, any day now..."

Sounds familiar, doesn't it? And if this is one of your best reps you'll probably believe it. But if not...well, who knows...What does "ninety percent" really mean? Are you both on the same page?

"Ninety percent" to the Sales Manager is usually interpreted as: "Good! We can count on getting this piece of business done by the end of this sales period-(whatever that is)." If accepted, this prediction could trigger all kinds of things; such are the ordering of raw materials, the hiring of additional staff, the creation of additional sales reports for the higher-ups and so forth.

To the Sales Rep, "ninety percent" often means: "Jeez! I gotta get this piece of business done now! The boss is counting on me... I sure hope that Mr. Prospect is going to come through for me..." [Remember the old sales joke about, "How do you tell when a prospect is lying to you? Answer: Their lips move."]

Over many years of experience I have come up with a list of what I call quantifiable "Confidence Factors." These are guidelines that help you, and sales management, make better guesses. I think they are pretty realistic and they are stringent, as they should be if we are going to be honest with one another.

Let's all get on the same page. Take a look at these Confidence Factors and see what you think. Go back and look at the far right hand column of Figure 4-A, "Confidence Factors:" you'll see three examples of how this works.

FIGURE 4-B

Confidence Factors for Accurate Forecasting

Factor %	Definition
100%	The order has been received, processed, and shipped during the last reporting period. The business has been booked.
90%	The order has been approved and signed off on by the client. The purchase order has been sent to us but not yet received. This business will be on the books in 30 days or less.
80%	The order has been approved by the client and the actual purchase document is in the process of being completed and sent to us. Documents will be in our hands during the next 30 days or less.
70%	The order has been agreed to and approved by all necessary parties. The actual purchase documents are not yet in process but should be in process during the next 30 days or less.
60%	The order had been agreed to but not all the required parties have signed off on the purchase. Final approval is nearing and should be granted in the next 30 days or less.
50%	The sale has been made conceptually: all parties agree that the purchase makes good sense. All required demos, phone tours, etc. have been completed. We are awaiting a final purchase decision. This go/no-go decision will be made in the next 30 days or less.
40%	We are in the advanced stages of striking a deal. Our sponsor is actively supporting the purchase. We need to gain more buy-in from all the key decision-makers and will get that within 30 days or less.
30%	We have a very interested and active prospect. We are discussing the features and benefits of all the products that would make a good fit for the customer. We anticipate that we will reach a decision to proceed or not to proceed within

30 days or less.

20%   We have a qualified prospect. We have done an initial sales analysis and it looks promising.

10%   We have a complete suspect. The suspect has some information on us or we have some information on them. We have, however, identified this suspect as someone we would like to work with.

TOOL # 4: The Sales Funnel: Let's talk some more about who makes it onto your "Top 25" list. With experience, you'll get to the point where your instincts alone can tell you who belongs there and who doesn't. But if you're new to the business, the company or the territory assigned to you; or, you've only been able to come up with eighteen entries for your list of twenty-five, how do you completely populate the list? One good way is to take all the rest of your "suspects" (unqualified raw sales leads or your scientific wild-ass guesses) and push them through the Sales Funnel. Like any good sieve, the Sale Funnel will keep the dross at the top and only squeeze out nectar at the bottom. The golden droplets that survive the pressing will make it onto your list of top prospects and customers.

The Sales Funnel example in Figure 4-C is from an on-line electronic learning company whose sales force I once supervised. There are twenty-five filters to this funnel. For your particular situation that may be too many. Perhaps you'll only need ten or fifteen, but reviewing this example will give you the ideas you will need to construct a sales funnel that will be perfect for your own particular use. In a way, it's a design sheet for the perfect prospect.

No matter how many filters you come up with, what you're looking for is a prospect that passes through at least half of them. The best prospects get through three-quarters or more. Prospects that don't seep down at least halfway are time-wasters and should be put aside for awhile. Maybe they'll mature with a little more aging.

I'm sure you're going to quickly see another real value to the Sales Funnel: in addition to filling up your Top 25 List it will save you a lot of wasted energy pursuing prospects that are going nowhere.

The Sales Funnel will also help you gauge how well you know your prospects. If you come up with a few "don't know" responses on a particular prospect it means you haven't done all the homework you need to do on this person or company and it's time to get some answers!

FIGURE 4-C SAMPLE SALES FUNNEL

THE SALES FUNNEL			
Fill out one of these forms for each of your prospects. Our BEST Prospects will have many if not all of the following attributes:			
	YES	NO	DON'T KNOW
1. An appreciation for the value of e-learning			
2. Budget readily available and committed for training			
3. Budget readily available and committed for training that includes e-learning			
4. A sense of urgency			
5. A need for products and/or services that are squarely in our area of expertise			
6. Identifiable internal champion			
7. The champion has influence or decision-making capability			
8. Has heard of us (in a positive light)			
9. Not affected by adverse economic conditions or at least willing to look beyond them			
10. Will understand an ROI analysis			
11. Willing to embrace new ideas/technologies			
12. Is constantly training (internal/external or both)			
13. Introduces new products frequently			
14. Time to market is a critical issue			
15. Has a CLO or Director of Training with e-learning experience or knowledge			
16. Looking for enterprise-wide solutions			
17. Champion is visionary or "evangelistic"			
18. Flexibility: realizes that technology is not always perfect			
19. Returns phone calls/e-mails			

20. Large org. with speed as a mantra/small-to-med. org. with desire to "get bigger"			
21. Our database of prospects IS their target audience			
22. Time-to-close is 90 days or less (on at least one sale)			
23. Little or no time to produce this type of work themselves			
24. Has already looked at competitor(s)			
25. Honest, straight-forward, approachable			
Total number of "Yes" responses			
20 or more "Yes" answers means a very viable prospect- a definite selection for your "Top 25"			
15-20 "Yes" answers means a very good prospect. Should be "worked" immediately			
10-15 "Yes" answers means questionable. Re-evaluate in 30 days			
Less than 10 "Yes" answers you are wasting your time			
If you have 4 or more "Don't Know" responses you don't know this prospect very well!			
It is your responsibility to get the information to push any "Don't Know" answers into the "Yes" or "No" column. As you can see,			
a small change of even 2 or 3 responses can put a prospect squarely into an actionable situation!			

TOOL # 5: The Plan Letter: It's actually quite rare for a salesperson to be in front of a qualified buyer at the exact moment the buyer needs to make a purchasing decision. The odds are about the same as walking into your local branch of The Department of Motor Vehicles and seeing every window full of agents eager to help you and there's no one in line but you!

It's much more typical for a salesperson to enter the prospect's or customer's current sales cycle somewhere before it is scheduled to conclude. It's also very common for buyers to not actually know when they should be making their purchasing decisions. I know that sounds a little strange, since making these types of decisions is what these people get paid for, but it happens. There could be lots of reasons: uncertainty about the economy, not having done all the research necessary, not knowing if they're getting the best price, not having clear direction from their own management, the list goes on and on. No matter what buyers or decision makers tell you the reason may be you have to remember that their lips are moving when they do!

If a buyer can't give you an order there's really only one reason: They aren't ready. If you really do want that order you will enhance your chances of getting it immensely if you show your prospects what they need to do to be ready. Many times they don't even know themselves what they need to do! This is what a Plan Letter is all about: you are going to be the "hero" and show them how to get where they need to be.

Now, in order to construct a great Plan Letter you are really going to need to do your homework. Since you've already taken this prospect though the Sales Funnel, placed them on your Top 25 List, given them some sort of Confidence Factor and possibly filled out a Blueprint (more on this in the next section), you already know a great deal about the prospect. This will make the writing of a Plan Letter a snap.

The sample Plan Letters in Figures 4-D and 4-E are two of the best I've seen. They are concise, knowledgeable, and helpful. Let me say something else about Plan Letters. You do not need to execute one for every sales situation. They are powerful tools but they take time and research. If you are regularly engaged in selling big ticket items with long sales cycles I'd expect you'd be writing Plan Letters more often than if you are in a high volume business with short sales cycles.

The Plan Letter is nothing more than hand-holding. It provides a visible, tangible roadmap for both you and your prospect to achieve a common goal: getting what you both need.

The Plan Letter also has several very powerful hidden benefits. It makes you look smart as hell to your prospect—and like a caring partner. The Plan Letter will also tell you if you're on the right track. If you've identified a goal or milestone that is off base, your prospect will tell you about it in a heartbeat. When tasks are committed to "paper" (these days usually via email or word processing) they become tangible and if they're wrong your prospect will jump on it because paper (real or electronic) has a nasty habit of creating a trail, and prospects don't like incorrect paper trails. Faced with issues committed to black-and-white prospects will now tell you things they were reluctant or not allowed to tell you before. This is very valuable info: it will allow you to correct any miscalculations or potential miss-steps you probably would have taken if you hadn't done a Plan Letter.

Another powerfully subtle benefit of the Plan Letter is that you are unconsciously beginning to get your prospect to say "Yes." If you look at my examples you'll see that each Plan Letter is asking a prospect to put their initials in the spaces where they are in agreement with The Plan. Even though each letter carefully, plainly and truthfully states that any initials or signatures are not contractual commitments in reality, what are you subliminally doing here? Yes! You guessed it! You're getting the prospect to say "Yes" to little steps that will lead up to the big step. You are getting your prospect in the habit of having a pen in hand to sign your ultimate purchase order.

This may be the most important subtlety of The Plan Letter: I can't tell you how many times I have had to ask for an order only to be re-buffed because the prospect wasn't ready: and the real bottom-line reason the prospect wasn't ready was only because they were afraid to make a mistake. The Plan Letter, if properly designed and agreed to by the sales pro and prospect, eliminates confusion and uncertainty and minimizes the potential for mistakes. Customers love that!

FIGURE 4-D
Sample Plan Letter #1

September 20, 2010

Mr. Big Prospect
BIG Enterprises, Inc.
300 South Street South
North Andover, MA 01845

Dear Mr. Prospect:

I am excited that we are working toward a solution for BIG Enterprises in regard to the integration of XYZ products and services and your marketing needs. Based on our discussion yesterday, I have drafted a suggested Adoption Plan and Implementation Schedule, which I have outlined below.

If I have your agreement on the dates and items in this plan, please initial each item. If we need to make changes to either the objectives or dates suggested, please contact me as soon as possible.

Objective	Target Date	Initials
1. Participate in a webcast demo	9-24	_____
2. Review membership package options (FYI-Intel recently signed up)	by 9-28	_____
3. Select membership package and review content details for XYZ Website	by 10-12	_____
4. Sign contract for membership package	by 10-19	_____
5. Schedule meeting for demo	by 10-3	_____
6. Send your materials to us for estimate	by 10-17	_____
7. Draft proposal for review	by 10-31	_____
8. Conduct demo at BIG	by 11-15	_____
9. Hold final proposal review	by 11-22	_____
10. Sign Contract	by 11-29	_____

11. Commence work	by 11-30	_____
12. Initial deployment for testing	by 12-15	_____
13. Products in place	by 12-20	_____

Your initials are **NOT** a contractual commitment. We will draft and sign a formal contract at the appropriate time. Your initials acknowledge that I have outlined the scope of the work correctly. This also presents you with an opportunity to modify any of the actions listed above.

Your initials do represent a serious interest in the products and services we have discussed. As a result, those initials allow me to begin to have resources within XYZ budgeted and scheduled for this project. This is crucial for delivery in a timely fashion.

Thanks for your support. I look forward to getting this project in motion and partnering with you on this and future endeavors.

Best Regards,

Salesperson
XYZ Corporation

FIGURE 4-E
Sample Plan Letter #2

May 17, 2011

Debra Sales Manager
Director, Strategic Marketing
BIG Bucks Internet Co.
910 East Avenue
Campbell, CA 95008

Dear Debra:

I am delighted that we are working toward a solution for Big Bucks in regard to the integration of XYZ products and services and your marketing needs. Based on our most recent meeting, I have outlined where I feel we have concurrence and how we might be of further service to you:

1. Schedule your four (4) Online Seminars, starting on September 19 and 21, 2009. This includes an e-mail invitation to 12,500 Designers, 12,500 Appliance Designers and up to 10,000 names from Big Bucks database. You do have the option of scheduling webcasts in May and June, utilizing our special promotional pricing.
If you agree with the above, please initial here:_____
Note:

- Our webcasts provide a collaborative forum for information exchange and can create excitement and demand for your latest products.
- What makes our webcasts different is that they provide you with the option to invite a selected group from our design engineering members and we can provide an archive of that webcast and track the participation and provide you with lead information. XYZ webcast technology was developed specifically to present technical content and allows for

"optimization" for the attendee to view every detail of your diagrams in your presentation.

2. We want to schedule a virtual lab demo so you can see the benefit of running a live webcast, and allowing interested attendees to sign up for an adjoining demonstration. In conjunction with your webcasts, Big Bucks can direct all attendees to a virtual lab which takes them, for instance, to an actual product interface.

If you agree with the above, please initial here:_____

Note:

- High-Impact demonstration-This provided a better experience for an engineer and dramatically improves the way you demonstrate your products and make them available for evaluation;
- A controlled experience- This allows the participant to later connect, for example, to a demo board to test equipment running under the control program, or they can import their own files to test your software product on their designs;
- Targeted sales leads- We monitor your virtual lab and provide you with the leads for anyone who tries your products.

3. Consider Big Bucks being featured on XYZ's website. We have created networks of technology-focused communities targeting the most significant areas of design activity today.

This area includes:

- What's new for today;
- Promote Online Webcasts-an announcement of your upcoming webcasts in September, or an archived webcast;
- Virtual Lab-feature an actual "test drive" of the new web server, for example. And, by hosting this lab, we provide you with the leads of anyone who tries your product.

If you agree with the above, please initial here:_____

4. Explore e-learning opportunities with XYZ. We help technology companies

move their product and component training to the web which is just-in-time and just-enough learning. We do this through:

- XYZ University-we could provide a course on the above products in conjunction with a virtual lab, or another custom course.
- A private campus where we develop specialized technical courses that become available only to BIG BUCKS employees or host your course on our web site in our XYZ University where it is available for thousands of engineers.

If you agree with the above, please initial here:_____

Debra, your initials represent that we want to proceed and represents the services we have discussed. If you are in agreement with the above, please acknowledge this by initialing the blocks above and faxing back this note to me at (310) 555-9999.

We can help BIG BUCKS reach a wider audience by taking advantage of our guild of qualified engineers, our marketing reach and our breadth of e-learning solutions. Thanks for your support and I look forward to talking with you again soon. Should you have any questions, you can always reach me at (310) 555-9999.

Regards,

Karen Salespro
Strategic Account Director
XYZ Corporation

TOOL # 6: The Blueprint for Success: It's pretty hard to build a house without a set of blueprints. In fact, in most locales a stamped, approved set of plans is a requirement before a single shovel full of dirt can be turned. You should build your "House of Sales" with a good blueprint, too. To that end, I'm including an outline for my ever-popular "Blueprint for Success: The Prospect to Client Checklist" (See Appendix 1). Two very important items before we get started on a discussion of this incredibly useful sales tool:

First and foremost, you must take this example blueprint and immediately re-draft it for your own purposes. Do not be intimidated by its everything-including-the-kitchen-sink length. I've given you everything you need to consider: add or subtract to get the best Blueprint for your own purposes.

Secondly, don't get carried away: Blueprints will take a lot of time and effort to produce. Reserve them for your very best customers and prospects. Do not begin filling out a Blueprint for a complete "suspect" or for every contact in your database. If you do that you'll spend more time on paperwork than selling.

OK, so what's the best way to use this Blueprint? It's a set of plans for turning your best prospects into loyal customers and it will help you look really smart and incredibly organized. When I was in the field selling, I'd bring along my Blueprints on my sales calls. It was very powerful when I sat down in front of a prospect, opened up my laptop with the prospect's Blueprint on screen and said something like, "Thanks for seeing me today. Now, here's what I know about you. I'd like to review this information and verify a few things about you and your company before we get to the real purpose for this meeting..." It never failed to blow every prospect away that (a) I had done my homework (b) cared enough to be intelligent about the prospect and (c) wasn't immediately hammering them with an uninformed sales pitch.

Let's go through a sample Blueprint (flip back-and-forth to Appendix 1):

Steps 1 and 2 are general background information and it's the minimal amount of information you should ever have before contacting an important prospect. You'll notice, I hope, that the Six Questions from earlier in this chapter are right up front. After you have completed Step 1 you should have a pretty good idea of why the heck you're chasing the prospect in the first place- or at least you should.

The information you need to complete Step 2 is the kind of data you can generally get form the company's website, a Google search, or any one of a number of facts-on-line websites such as Wikipedia.

Step 3: This step documents everything relative to your initial sales call with this prospect. The example is set up to assist you with a face-to-face meeting, but it can easily be adapted for a teleconference, webinar, or scheduled conference call. Step 3 is where you make that all-important first impression. If you blow this, you're in a hole and constantly trying to dig yourself out; so, do your homework (Steps 1 and 2) and rehearse Step 3 before you get in front of this prospect.

You will see right at the beginning of Step 3 that we clearly state the purpose of this initial call: we're not going in guns blazing, mowing down objections and pressing them for an order. If this prospect is big enough and important enough to require the completion of a Blueprint (a) this is not a first call close situation, and (b) you're hoping to get something truly spectacular out of this prospect so stay focused. Follow each step carefully!

Your main objectives in Step 3 are:

a.) to put the prospect at ease
b.) to look caring, intelligent, and professional
c.) to confirm:
    i) the decision maker (s)
    ii) that they have money
    iii) that they will spend it
    iv) when it will be spent
d.) uncover their most pressing needs
e.) begin matching those needs to your solutions
f.) begin to gently sell yourself and your solutions

Most importantly, you will not have a successful initial call unless you both know and agree on the next step in the process.

Step 4: This is the time to reflect on the initial call. How serious is this prospect? Where does this prospect fall in relation to how much work you want to put into this prospect right now? What are the most important issues? How does your company's product line fit the issues? Step 4 is a snap judgment on the initial sales call and should be completed as soon as possible after that call-- maybe even in the parking lot outside the prospect's office.

Step 5: This is reflection after the parry and thrust of the initial sales call. It is done after you get back to your office when you can flesh out the reactions to the initial sales call with a little more science.

Step 6: Based on what you know now, you can intelligently look at the potential for doing business with this prospect and one of the best ways to do this is to try and parse out what you think the prospect's main objections are at this point. Is your price point too high? Will the prospect have to re-tool? Are there significant training challenges? Whatever you think the objections might be, write them down and begin to think about what you are going to do: what resources you can bring to bear? What kind of plan can you devise that will overcome the objections?

Step 7: You are now at the Initial or Trial Close stage. Take your notes, guesses on objections, suggested solutions and ideas back to the prospect and validate them—or not. I suggest that this step be done face-to-face, just like Step 3, but in this electronic age, it doesn't necessarily need to be. The ultimate goals of Step 7 are:
  a.) validation of your premises and clearing up of any confusion
  b.) the creation of a plan of action (Plan Letter?)

Now, it's entirely possible, and it does happen from time to time, that you have been so effective and impressive that your trial close will become a real close. If so, for heaven's sake stop! You're done! Skip to Step 10: A little further on I will relate to you an amusing story about a sales rep I knew who got a big close at Step 7 and tried to push to Step 8 anyway!
  If you're not lucky enough to close at Step 7 (it'll only happen ten percent of the time) go on to:

Step 8: "Plan your work and work your plan." During Step 8 you are continually updating your Blueprint, working with the prospect to overcome all objections and making sure all the milestones in your Plan Letter are being accomplished. If you are doing all this correctly you are also tossing subtle trial closes at the prospect all the time. When all the goals are accomplished and the Plan complete you will (or should) get an acceptance and a deal. Congratulations! Move on to:

Step 9: Handshakes are great, but signatures are better. Get the paperwork done. At least get an agreement on a plan to the get the paperwork done.

Step 10: Done deal, right? Wrong! Cynically, the deal isn't done until your commission check clears the bank. The message is this: I have seen "done deals" come unglued more times than I care to remember because either the prospect, the salesperson or both forgot to dot all the "i's" and cross all the "t's." Keep on it until everything is in place! Also, learn from your experiences. Write out the lessons you've learned, what you might have done differently. It'll shorten your sales cycle with the next big prospect.

The Six Questions, The Top 25 List, Confidence Factors, The Sales Funnel, The Plan Letter, and the Blueprint for Success are the best sales tools I have ever come across. They all work together, too, by the way, and they all mesh seamlessly, one into the other. You don't have to deploy them all and you'll certainly want to adapt the ones you have seen in this book to your own use, but not using a tool kit would make anyone's job a lot tougher. Not using any of these tools will make your sales life darn near impossible.

CHAPTER 5: THE MOST COMMON PITFALLS—THEY ALL GUARANTEE FAILURE:

Just as there are certain positive steps sales people can take that will practically ensure success there are landmines that will always guarantee failure. I don't want to dwell on the negatives but the pitfalls that I am going to mention now are common, pervasive and utterly avoidable.

Falling in Love with "Yes!": Sales people are pretty much prepared for rejection, or at least they should be, and if you can't handle rejection you don't belong in sales. Really good sales people brush off rejections and either keep plowing ahead, refuse to be defeated or choose to move on to the next possibility. What sales people are hardly ever prepared for is something I have come to call "fake acceptance." There are buyers and prospects that are not hard-nosed bad asses. (Yes, I know, hard to believe, isn't it?) Actually there are prospects out there that are gentle, meek, self-effacing or so in need of being perceived as nice that they will "yes" salespeople to death. Frankly, I prefer the "bad-asses." "Yes People" are much harder to work: they waste your time, string you along, give you false hopes and lie like rugs.

Since there is nothing a salesperson likes to hear more than "yes," it's quite natural for salespeople to fall in love with "yes" and let the "Yes People" overwhelm them. I ran across a chronic "Yes Person" early in my sales career and she damn near drove me to drink. She was an Assistant Superintendent of Schools for Curriculum and Instruction from a fairly large suburban school district in Southern California. She was an ex-teacher, a perfectly lovely lady, professional, caring, pleasant and oh-so-nice.

Her challenge was quite typical: to take limited budget and get the most she could for the money the school board had already set aside for computer-based instruction. At the time, there were half a dozen premier companies competing in this relatively narrow field. Frankly, all of my competitors had good product that was fairly priced. What made the real difference between my company and any of the others was service and support. Fortunately, my firm was a significant cut above in this category.

From the moment I first walked into "Ms. Yes" office I was greeted warmly and made to feel right at home. It was her breathless "I'm so glad you came" and "Where have you been?" attitude that lulled me into believing this was going to be a slam-dunk. At every step in the sales process she enthusiastically and eagerly said "Yes!" Every one of my product demonstrations was a winner. Every meeting with staff and teachers was positive. Every administrator and board member was smiling and nodding approval. Ms. Yes got to know my product so well she could sell it almost as well as I could. She even baked cookies for some of our meetings! I was counting the days until I could cash my big, fat commission check. The "yeses" went on and on.

And then I realized one cold and utterly devastating day that this was exactly what was wrong: there was never a "no," a roadblock or an expressed objection--nothing but "yeses." But nothing was happening! I began to panic then I finally woke up. I had fallen so in love with hearing "yes," I couldn't even see the "no's" that were obviously blocking this deal. Here were the questions I finally asked that made it all clear to me. Please pay close attention to how they were answered by Ms. Yes:

Me: "So, when can we actually sit down and sign the contracts that will complete our deal?"

Ms. Yes: "Why yes, we certainly will have to do that at some point, won't we?

Me: "Yes, we will. Can we do it today?"

Ms. Yes: "I'm certain we'll be able to conclude something very soon."

Me: "How soon?"

Ms. Yes: "Just as soon as I get the additional agreements I need among the teachers and administrators."

Me: "When might that be?"

Ms. Yes: "I'm sure it won't take long. We're just a yes or two away!"

And so it went. I did a little digging. I had some friends among the competition. We all knew each other: we all went to the same trade shows, conferences and sales people gin joints. Much to my shock and amazement no fewer than three of my close competitors firmly believed that they were going to close this deal. Ms. Yes had given each of them the same assurances she had given me.

The good news is that my company finally did get a contract but it wasn't for another six months and only after "Ms. Yes" was given another assignment in the district by her boss. I fell in love with "yes' and got burned for quite some time. The lesson is this: just because your prospect says "yes" to you it does not mean the deal is done. You must have a process by which you can dispassionately decide when a sale is truly concluded (more on this later.)

Lying to Yourself: if you can lie to yourself you can lie to anyone.

We've already touched on honesty as being one of the key characteristics of successful sales people. This is the polar opposite and one sure-fire way to be unsuccessful in sales. People lie for all kinds of reasons. I even read a scholarly piece of psychoanalytic research recently that argued that not telling the whole truth can sometimes be better than being totally truthful. One example given was telling people with dangerously low self-esteem that they are not as unattractive as they truly are. In this case lying, even just a little, to give a wretched personality some hope was deemed better than telling them, "Boy, you are one ugly son-of-a-bitch."

I am not here to argue the moral aspects of lying versus telling the truth. For more on that you can consult a veritable library of books on the subject. I'm here to tell you that the practical, everyday policy of trying to kid yourself will produce very limited--if any--results, especially in sales.

When you start saying things to yourself like:

"I'll get that sales report done later when I have more time."

"I can't cold call today. I really don't need to anyway."

"They'll never realize their shipment is twelve units short. They'll never miss them."

"I can pad this contract with an extra $5000 and increase my commission $500. No one will be the wiser."

"They've got more money than they know what to do with. I'm going to tweak the price."

"I can swap the '07 widgets for the '08's and save my company a ton. They'll never know the difference."

You're lying to yourself which means you'll lie to anybody and everybody.

Lying to Management: There are really only a few reasons salespeople lie to sales management or higher-ups in the company:
-to buy time
-to cover up a mistake
-to look good (or better) than they are
None of these reasons are justifiable. They will always start a spiral toward implosion and self destruction. I have never, ever seen or experienced a salesperson getting canned for telling the truth. Disciplined, maybe, or slapped on the wrist if they made a stupid mistake, but never fired. I certainly wouldn't fire anyone for telling the truth but on the other hand I've had to fire too many people for lying to me. It's just stupid. Don't do it.

Not Listening: Too many salespeople think that they have to talk incessantly in order to be successful. Too many salespeople believe they can brow-beat their prospects into submission with a ceaseless stream of sales chatter. Conjure up in your own mind the very worst images of the most obnoxious salespeople you've ever run across. Aren't they the ones who never shut up? Prospects and customers like to be listened to as much as they like to be sold. If you're not listening and if you're not being truly empathetic, you're not going to be very successful. Two examples from real life:

I went into a sales situation with a rookie sales rep once where I was there just to provide backup. After the obligatory meet-and-greet we settled down to some serious product talk. The rookie began his spiel and plowed on through thirty minutes of material that was actually pretty good. The problem was this: had the rookie been listening instead of just selling he would have picked up that the software that he was there to sell would never be compatible with the hardware systems the prospect was using. We didn't find this out until after it was all over and the prospect said, "Gee this sounds just like what we need! This is great! And it runs on our "X" hardware platform, right?" No, it didn't. We looked like the idiots we were.

Here's the alternate universe version, also from real life, and I was privileged to witness this one:

A relatively new but sharp sales rep and I walk into a meeting to try and sell our software solution to a lady who, in our business, was known as a hard negotiator but very knowledgeable. Once again, pleasantries are exchanged. The buyer gets right to the point and takes ten minutes to explain to us what she needs. The sales rep goes into serious listening mode. At the right moments he happens to ask a couple of pretty intelligent questions that help direct the discussion. Our buyer finally concludes her laundry list of needs and wants. The sales rep (I trained him, of course!) simply says, "We can do that." Four little words, that's all. The buyer says, "Well, if you can then we have a deal." How sweet was that? All accomplished mostly by good listening.

"Premature Elaboration:" I always get a chuckle out of this topic when I lay it on the sales training table. It goes with the "not listening" topic above but yet it's a little different. We're consistently telling our sales people to talk about features and benefits. We tell sales trainees to be sure the prospects clearly understand what it is we have to sell and all the wonderful things our products will do for them. What we don't tell them is how to know when it's time to shut the hell up and transition to trying to close the sale or let the prospect talk. I have seen bright sales people so eager to sell, so anxious to do a good job that they sometimes miss the signals that say "Stop, it's my turn;" or, "OK, I'm ready to deal." To these folks the sales process sometimes overwhelms the need to listen. They are guilty of "premature elaboration." I have a story to illustrate this point. It happened to me years ago and I've never tired of telling the tale:

I was in a rural school district on the eastern shore of Maryland. My sales rep covering the territory was a wonderful young lady, new to sales, but very sharp, very personable and eager to please. She asked me to come in and help her with a possible contract with large potential. She felt she was ready to try and close this school district but she wanted some moral support from me. I was glad to accept. The strategy was simple: we were taking the superintendent of schools to lunch at his favorite restaurant along with his deputy superintendent for curriculum and instruction. My rep was fairly convinced that the four of us, over a convivial lunch, could conclude a deal. I knew she had done her homework. We were both confident that most if not all the objections had been asked and answered.

The four of us sat down at a table by the window with a glorious view of the water. It was a balmy, pleasant spring day. The moon and the stars seemed to be in alignment. We chatted, ordered our lunch, and had just begun to dig into the appetizers when the serious discussions began. My sales rep had been up until the wee hours preparing for this and she was locked and loaded. She waded right in, just as I had taught her, and began to review all the features and benefits that were sure to seal the deal.

The superintendent stopped, a perfect shrimp two inches from his mouth. He interrupted my sales rep and calmly said to her, "You can stop right there. I'm going to sign your contract this afternoon. You've done a great job for us; now enjoy your lunch as much as I'm going to enjoy mine."

I still have a hard time believing what my sales rep said next:

"No! Wait! I'm not done."

It was all I could do not to kick her under the table. She had prepared this elaborate set of arguments and counter arguments and she was not about to be deterred. We all stopped, frozen in time.

She was about to continue full-force into her prepared speech when I leaned over and whispered in her ear, "Yes. You are done. Now eat your soup!"

This is, perhaps, an extreme example of my point, but it's too good a story not to tell! I have seen "premature elaboration" more often on the front end of a possible deal. It occurs whenever selling starts before the listening is done.

Not Asking for the Order: This is the single most common characteristic of unsuccessful sales people. All the careful preparation, listening, smiling and overcoming of objections in the world is useless if you can't ask for (and get) the order. I have never understood why this is so hard to do yet time and time again I have seen otherwise talented sales people go 95 % of the way toward a successful sale then fail to pull the trigger. My guess is that not asking for the order is likely an extension of our natural fear of rejection, yet rejection is just another part of the sales process. We love to hear "yes" and we naturally hate to hear "no;" so, how to get beyond it? The best way, I think, is to come up with whatever way is most comfortable for you to ask for the order. Here are some good examples:

"So, have we reached that point where we can get serious and begin concluding a transaction? (If not, you'll certainly hear about it!)

"I'd like to see you get (these products) into (your warehouse) before (Christmas). Can we work up some purchase orders today?

"We've got a lot of work to do to get these (products) into (your factories) so they can make a difference. Let's get started by drafting the contracts today."

"I hope I've gained your trust and confidence through the sales process we've been through; now, I'd love to have your business."

Don't be "cute":

"I got my order pad all warmed up and ready to go!"

Don't be overly aggressive:

"If you want that discount price you gotta act today!"

Don't be stupid:

"There are two tickets to the Super Bowl in it for you if you sign today!"

Don't beg:

"Please! I need this deal to make my quota for the month!"

It's OK to be firm, exact and precise but you must at all times be professional.

"If I've earned your respect, I'm pleased. If I've also moved you to place an order, I'm also proud."

[FYI: We're going to discuss this trait in much more depth in the next chapter.]

E-Mail Jail: The proliferation of the Internet with all its promise and capabilities can provide fabulous sales opportunities but it also contains traps for the unwary. The worst of these traps is a time-waster I call "E-Mail Jail." E-mail has become so pervasive and so demanding that it can become counter-productive. If we're not careful we're going to become slaves to a tool that was originally meant to help us become more efficient and more communicative. When there are just so many contact opportunities in a selling day and your day starts with: "Bing! You have 103 unread e-mails," how are you going to stay focused and remain productive?

Answers to this quandary are still being sought but I would submit to you it's time to go back to the 80/20 rule (see Chapter 3): 80 percent of your serious e-mails will come from 20 % of those sent to you; 80 % of any business you conclude via the Internet will come from 20% of your Internet contacts; 80% of your e-mails will waste your time and energies, 20% of them will be truly important. Well, you can do the math on this one by yourselves by now.

Forgetting Who Brought you to the Dance: I love this expression. The vulgar version, straight out of a Texas Two-Step Honky-Tonk is more like: "Be sure to go home with the one who brung ya." In any sales cycle with any prospect there is always someone who got you there to start. Don't forget them. It could cost you. Perhaps it's a referral from a trade show contact. It could even be from a competitor! If the contact results in a sale it's time to go back and thank "The one who brung ya." What's an appropriate recognition for getting you into the deal? Be sure you know what your company's compliance policies are before sending champagne, a new Rolex or offering commission splits. Phone calls, e-mails and greeting cards with a simple "Thank you" are always in good taste.

Failing to Understand the Whole Sales Cycle: I fault sales trainers for this poor habit more than I do sales people. We rarely spend enough time analyzing our own company's sales cycles and many times, even when we do, we fail to impart this critical knowledge to our own sales staff. If your sales execs can't lay out the whole process for you, form cold-call to closed deal, you start with one hand tied behind your back. Do yourself—and your boss—a favor: sit down and chart it out. Then use it! Oh, did I mention we already discussed a good tool for this? Remember the "Blueprint" discussion in Chapter 3?

CHAPTER 6: THE ALL-IMPORTANT CLOSE:

The one character trait that seems to truly differentiate between those who are "born to sell" and those who are not, is the ability to seal the deal. Natural born sales people will always ask for the order. They will be closing constantly. It's something true sales people don't' even have to worry about doing even if they sometimes need some help in understanding how to do it. On the flip side, just like cold-calling, closing strikes terror in the hearts of those who should not be in sales.

The use of the web as a sales tool has made life a little easier for those who are engaged in on-line sales. First, there are billions of potential customers, many of whom will come back time and again so there's no lack of potential closing opportunities. Second, the somewhat impersonal nature of e-commerce takes a bit of the sting of rejection out of the picture. It's much less threatening to get an impersonal "no thanks" e-mail than it is to look in someone's eyes and have them say "no" to you.

I have watched many sales people, sometimes in horror, sometimes in amusement; do everything in their power to avoid closing. For those who are fearful of rejection the close is that last step in getting the door slammed in your face (literally or figuratively). Not wanting to get to that last step is understandable for these people. True sales people, however, can't wait to get to an opportunity to ask for the order.

How do you know when the time is right? Sometimes it's fairly obvious. For the retail jewelry sales person watching a potential customer lovingly fondle the expensive watch he's been looking at for fifteen minutes the question becomes, "Can I box that up for you?" If the same customer's still musing over three potential watches, then you still have some more work to do. In this case, you would attempt what we call a "trial close."

In a trial close you're trying to get the prospect to make a decision—

any decision. Sometime it works, sometimes it doesn't but the very least you should get out of trying to close is to get the potential buyer to narrow the options. In the example of our jewelry patron still agonizing over three choices you might say something like, "I see you like all three of these watches. Which one best fits your lifestyle? Which one says 'that's me!'?" This type of questioning might get the customer to focus on what's really meaningful and prompt a decision.

At the very least you want a trial close to help you overcome any remaining objections to an actual close. In a face-to-face sales scenario you might hear something like this:

Salesperson: "So, we agree that we've got the right storage batteries for your new line of electric lawn mowers, how many can I ship to you?" (Trial close!)

Purchasing Agent: "None right now. I'm not ready. Come back and see me in a month."

The non-professional salesperson will say to himself/herself, "Whew! I'm outta here! That was tough but I didn't get a 'no.' I'll come back in a month for a big sale!"

A true sales professional will understand that the trial close hasn't worked and will continue probing to try and overcome the hidden objection.

Salesperson: "When you say you're not ready does that mean you don't need the batteries now?"

Purchasing Manager: "Oh, no. I definitely need the batteries and you've given me a good price but my warehouse is full. I don't have any place to store them!"

(Now you've uncovered the real problem.)

Salesperson: "Well, if we strike a deal now so you can get this excellent price I'll hold off on delivery, until you tell me to send them. Would that be OK?"

Purchasing Manager: "Perfect! You've got a deal!"

Trial close-probe-response: do that over and over until you get to the bottom line objection. Once you do, you can close the sale-or at least truly understand why you can't and what you need to do to get there.

Sometimes it's just bizarre. I remember a prospect from my early software selling days that desperately needed what I had to sell. We went at it hammer and tong, in a pleasant way, for over an hour one day. I trial-closed time and again, uncovering all possible objections and coming back with reasonable responses every time. She kept saying "No." We sat there like two punch drunk fighters at the end of the 12th round. I finally asked her the one last question I could think of: "Jane, you need this. You want this and you have the money for it. Why won't you just buy it?" Her answer was shocking but it finally got me to the last hurdle. She looked me right in the eye and said, "Because I don't like you."

What could I say to that?! The only think I could think of, and it was an act of desperation was, "So, if I send in another sales rep from my company you'll do the deal?" Her answer was, "Yes." I sent in another rep form the adjoining sales territory, she got a signature and we split the commission. Half a loaf is better than none-but I never found out why she didn't like me!

Trial closes are extremely useful, but be careful. There are buyers out there who like to toy with sales people just for the fun of it. To some it's a cat-and-mouse game and guess who the rodent is: you! You don't see this too much anymore because the world has gotten a lot busier and much more professional, but it can happen. If you suspect that the potential buyer is dangling cheese in front of your face instead of a deal just ask him or her in a playful manner, "I bet you're good at playing poker too, but all my chips are on the table and I'm calling for your order, so, what'll it be?"

Humor is a powerful tool. I'm not talking about telling jokes. I'm suggesting that you have a few funny comebacks prepared like the poker player above. It can help reduce the tension of a final negotiation session. For example, in a scenario where price is an issue I have used this one (and you can change the dollar amount to suit your needs):

Prospect: "So, what's this program going to cost me?"
Salesperson: (Actual cost was $100,000.00)
"Substantially less than a million dollars."

The prospect was initially shocked. He knew as well as I did that a million was about ten times the real price. Then he chuckled and I knew I had him. First, the humor helped break the ice. Secondly, subtlety and psychologically he was relieved it wasn't going to cost him a million dollars and suddenly one hundred thousand didn't seem like such a big deal.

As there are purchasers who like to play the cat with sales people there are also those who like to be the mouse. Some buyers, believe it or not, like being told what to do. They are typically so busy or so distracted that it's a relief to have their minds made up for them. If you know how to ask for the order this will be an easy sale.

Buyer: "I just don't know. It seems like you have the right product but I just can't decide."

Salesperson:" I tell you what we'll do (note: The powerful use of the word "we".) I'll put in an order for an initial supply and you can try the first batch. If they work as I have described we'll order more. If they don't, you still have our money back guarantee. So, let's get started shall we?"

Buyer: "Well, OK, that sounds good to me."

If you don't ask for the order in this case there will be two people wandering around in the dark accomplishing nothing! But you must be careful: buyers like this are easy targets and the temptation to take advantage could be powerful. Stay the course, be honest and doing the right thing.

The majority of buyers, of course, are neither cats nor mice. They simply want to be convinced that they are going to receive value for their money. They want nothing more than an even exchange of their resources for something they need and value. They will not give in easily and they will- and should- ask lots of questions. It's your job as a sales professional to answer all the questions honestly and straightforwardly. The real test comes when all the buyer's questions are asked and answered: do you have the strength to ask for the order and, if you do, to overcome any remaining objections?

If you go to the doctor and say, "I have a stomach ache." The doctor does not typically say, "You have stomach cancer. We'll schedule surgery for tomorrow at 9 a.m. and follow up with six months of chemotherapy." Rather, one would hope the doctor would begin with an external examination and ask lots of questions.

Sales people have to be like good doctors. If the prospect says they can't "stomach" (ouch!) your deal you have to start probing and asking lots of questions. Remember: trial close—probe—uncover objections—overcome objections—close again. Keep doing this over and over until the deal is done. If you have done your homework and are in front of a qualified prospect with the means and ability to consummate a sale my guess is that eight times out of ten (the 8/20 rule, remember?) you'll get a deal. Even if you don't get a contract you will, at the very least, understand why you didn't get a deal. Although this will not put any immediate money in your pocket it will help fill up your store of knowledge and that will make you an even better salesperson.

Even in the land of "NO!" there is money to be made. There were times in my career when "No" meant "no deal." Before I walked away, however, I always asked one last question: "Even though we couldn't reach an agreement, is there someone else you could recommend that I talk with?" In a surprising number of cases I got referrals that resulted in sales.

CHAPTER 7: SERVICE, SERVICE, SERVICE...

You've probably heard it before: in real estate, the three most important factors are "location, location, location." It's true and the sales corollary is: "service, service, service."

When I conduct sales training I am often asked, "When is a sale really done?" My response is always the same: "A sale is not complete until the person you have sold refers someone else to you who also buys." In my mind, this scenario completes the sales cycle. What it implies, of course, is that you have given such a complete level of sales, support and service that your happy buyer is putting you in front of other friends and colleagues. There can be no higher compliment than this for any sales professional.

I did not learn this lesson in business; I actually learned it first in the military. Right after I joined my first squadron, deployed aboard the aircraft carrier *USS Constellation*, I was designed the Weapons Office. As "WEPS" one of my many duties was to make sure the bombs were loaded. In the middle of a very intense period of fighting in Vietnam two of my critical weapons loaders went down: one with pneumonia, the other with a crushed foot after a 500-pound bomb fell on his ankle. I could have sat back and bitched to my Commanding Officer or I could have pitched in. I decided to strip off my officer's tunic and hump bombs with the rest of my men. Twelve back-breaking hours later we got the job done. My CO was so impressed with my "can-do" spirit he actually wrote me an official Letter of Commendation. It taught me a great lesson on service and support that I carried forward into my business career: You cannot give enough service and the increases in your business will be directly reflective of the amount of service you give.

Do you have to make "friends" with your customers? No, getting too friendly can, in and of itself, become a slippery slope. It's best to be professional and leave it at that. What you do want your customers to say is, "Man, the service I get, well, it's just outstanding!"

Service is professionalism. Service is simply the right thing to do. But here's the real secret: Service (=) Trust. When you serve your customers to the best of your ability they will trust you and when they trust you they will continue to buy from you. They will also recommend and refer you. It will be hard for your competitors to break into your circle of satisfied customers.

There is, however, just a little bit of a caution, and here comes the ol' 80/20 rule yet again. You cannot, all of a sudden, begin to spend 80% of your time on service and 20% on selling! You've got to keep your eye on the prize which is selling (80%) and giving great service (20%).

CHAPTER 8: WHAT IT ALL MEANS:

Sales can be an enormously gratifying profession, not to mention a lucrative one. I firmly believe, as I stated at the beginning of this book, that great sales people are "naturals." Sometimes they shine brilliantly form the start. More often than not they are diamonds-in-the-rough that need to be discovered then cleaned, cut and polished.

There are many excellent books, papers, and websites on selling and the craft of selling. There are lots of great seminars and sales training tools out there, too. What I have attempted to do in this brief treatise is to give you a simple frame of reference for the sales profession. Now that you know you were meant to be in sales and now that you have been armed with the very best baseline sales tools and successful sales characteristics, you are better prepared to take advantage of some of the more comprehensive skill building programs. I certainly encourage you to try them. Sales is a career-long learning process and one that should never stop.

Sales is one of the great professions. Never think otherwise and never let anyone tell you differently. The person who ultimately finds the cure for cancer will have bought the electron microscope, chemicals, surgical supplies and computers needed to develop that cure from salespeople who knew enough about their craft to put the right tools in the right hands. The world leaders who sign the peace treaties will use conference tables appropriate to the occasions supplied by sales people who put the right furniture in the right place at the right time. Melodramatic? Perhaps. But when your child skins a knee and needs ointment and a band-aid be thankful for your local pharmacy sales rep. As I said in the beginning: "Nothing happens until somebody sells something." To that I now add, "Nothing **CAN** happen until somebody sells something."

For those of you who take up the order pad, I wish you good luck and good selling!

APPENDIX 1
Blueprint for Success
Prospect-to-Client Checklist

STEP 1- PROSPECT BACKGROUND

Date:

Prospect:_____

Initial Contact:_____

Phone:_____email:_____

Website:_____

Primary Sponsor:_____

WHO developed the contact?_____

HOW was the initial contact developed?_____

WHEN was the initial contact made?_____

WHAT was the reason for the initial contact?_____

_____

WHERE was the prospect developed?_____

WHY was the contact made?_____

Your perception of the prospect's initial needs:_____

_____

_____

_____

_____

_____

_____

_____

_____

STEP 2- GATHERING PROSPECT INFORMATION

When was the company founded? Brief history, background:_____

_____

_____

_____

Type (circle):   C-corp. S-corp. LLC   Partnership Other:_____

Owner(s):_____

Company Leadership:

Pres/CEO:_____

Senior VP (s):_____

CFO:_____

Other Senior Officers to know:_____

_____

What is the principal line of business?:_____

Are there any other subsidiaries? Divisions? Locations?

_____

_____

What are current annual sales? Last year? Year before?

_____

_____

STEP 3-THE INITIAL CALL*

First call actual date:_____Person(s) called on:_____

_____

[*The purpose of which is NOT to sell your products: it is to gather the data you need to begin to sell your products!]

Pre-Call Checklist:(You should have, at minimum, the following items with you-but NO MORE!)

Business Cards

Media Kit (for all attendees, plus five)

Your appointment book

This blueprint (for note taking)

Brochures for any upcoming conferences/meetings, trade shows, etc.

(Anything more than this is too much. Your goal is to identify needs, decision makers and schedule a second call!)

Initial meeting checklist: ALL of the following, at minimum, should be discussed (check them off as you complete them) but the flow and order should go with your discussion:

Introductions/Business Cards
Why you're there ("to gather information- not to sell")
How you got there

Note: Very little if any product info should be discussed at this point unless prospect directs you there. You can't intelligently discuss your product line until you know what your prospect needs! For the next few minutes direct the discussion to focus on the needs of the prospect.

"Tell me a little about the company" (verify initial information)

_____

_____

_____

_____

Decision Maker (purchases):_____

_____

Any others ("besides yourself") involved in approval and purchase process?:

_____

# of Employees in dept.:_____Other locations:_____
Types of programs/products currently being used/run (and titles if known):

_____

_____

_____

What is the budget for purchases during the next 12 months?
        $_____
How much of the budget will be spent in this type of product?:

_____

Is this budget firmly committed?_____
Are you looking at any particular programs now?_____

_____

Are you talking to any other companies or other program suppliers or resellers?

_____

_____

_____

What are the your most pressing needs/problems. Develop five: (These should be the company's most critical issues-and they may or may not relate to your products or services.)

1. _____
2. _____
3. _____
4. _____
5. _____

(Note: this "hot list" becomes your point of departure for directing rest of discussion. Now YOU begin to take control.)

Now develop a "wish list." "If you could design the product best suited to your needs (omitting, for the moment, cost considerations) what would it look like?"

1. _____   6. _____
2. _____   7. _____
3. _____   8. _____
4. _____   9. _____
5. _____   10. _____

"Anything else I should know?"

_____
_____
_____

Now you can begin the sales process. Using the notes you have just created, go directly to a brief overview of your products that most closely fit the "hot list" and "wish list" points. Show you can help.

Closure: Goal is to develop a plan for future action at this time, at this meeting. Schedule next meeting: Goal is a product presentation or closing session with key decision makers.

- Date of next meeting
- Products to be demonstrated
- Media to be used for demo
- Support/materials to be sent prior to first product presentation
- Who will coordinate presentation for prospect?
- Anything else?
- Thanks! Materials delivery

Meeting notes:

_____

_____

_____

_____

STEP 4- INITIAL CALL ASSESSMENT
Temperature of prospect (circle one)
        Immediate buyer
        Buyer within six months
        Within one year
        Long term prospect
        Low interest/ability*
* In which case you have finished the blueprint on this prospect, and you file it.
Mark it to be reviewed in six months.

Five most important issues and your solutions:
1. _____
Solution:_____
2. _____
Solution:_____
3. _____
Solution:_____
4. _____
Solution:_____
5. _____
Solution:_____

Does the prospect need: (check all that apply)
Custom work____
Consulting_____
Product courses and lectures_____
(Your products here):_____
(Your products here):_____
(Your products here):_____

Partner products/services (describe):

_____

_____
Other:_____

STEP 5-REASSESSMENT
You are now about the mid-point of a typical strategic sale. (Where are you?)
Date: _____   What is the next step?_____
What are the goals now:_____
What has changed significantly?_____

_____
What are your sales expectations? Revenue total?_____

_____
Closing date?_____
What are the current roadblocks to a signed contract?_____

_____
Key sponsor now (who has ownership at prospect level)?_____

_____
e-mail:_____ Phone:_____

Conflicts Resolution: What resources do you need to bring to bear now to help
you? (check all that apply):

Sales management_____   References_____

Finance_____   Tech Support_____

Visitation (to corporate)_____ Bids and Proposals_____

Pricing_____   Other___ _____

STEP 6-OVERCOMING OBJECTIONS
List all objections to signed contract and how to overcome them.

1.Objection: _____
        Counter:_____
2.Objection: _____
        Counter:_____
3.Objection: _____

Counter:_____
4.Objection: _____
      Counter:_____
5.Objection: _____
      Counter:_____
6.Objection: _____
      Counter:_____
7.Objection: _____
      Counter:_____
8.Objection: _____
      Counter:_____
9.Objection: _____
      Counter:_____
10.Objection: _____
      Counter:_____

STEP 7- INITIAL CLOSE

You now go back to your sponsor(s) (by phone or in person) and sit down and review objections/roadblocks. You offer your solutions. At this session, you put together a plan (plan letter) to overcome objections, implement solutions, assign milestone dates to complete you goals and responsibility.

              Date to complete
Goal 1 _____
Goal 2 _____
Goal 3 _____
Goal 4 _____
Goal 5 _____

The last lines of your plan are always:
Date to complete:
Final presentation:
Bid/Contract Prep date:
Final Approval date:
Contract Signing date:

Initial Installment(s) begin date:
Plan Letter sent on:

STEP 8- WORKING TOWARD THE CLOSE
WORK YOUR PLAN!
Review all info and keep it updated. When all objections have been overcome, and plan milestones are complete, you are ready for Step 9.

STEP 9-THE CLOSE AND CONTRACT SIGNING
- (Final) Presentation Date: _____
- Who will you need at the meeting: _____
  _____

- Proposal requested Date: _____
- Expected Approval Date: _____

Bid/Contract Preparation:
Finance review:_____
Bid release date:_____
Bid response due date:_____
Bid/Contract review complete: _____
Bid opening date: _____
Contract signing date: _____
Final approval date:_____
Contract in hand date:_____
Amount: $_____

Time of completion, Start (step 1) to Finish:_____

STEP 10-THE ALL IMPORTANT FOLLOW-UP
(check-off as completed)
___Contract to corporate (date)_____
___Vendor Partners contacted (if any)
___Pre-install meetings coordinated (date)_____
___Implementation schedule done

___Hold pre-install meetings

___Product in-place (date)_____

___I have asked for referrals

___I will remember to keep clients updated

___I will show additional products

Why did you succeed, in the final analysis, with this client?

_____

_____

_____

What would you have done differently?

_____

_____

LESSONS LEARNED:

1. _____

2._____

3._____

4._____

5._____

BIO FOR PHIL KEITH:

Phil has a degree in History from Harvard and has done Masters Work at the Naval War College and Long Island University. After graduation from Harvard Phil went directly into the Navy and became a Naval Aviator. During three tours in Vietnam Phil served with distinction and was awarded, among other decorations, the Air Medal for Gallantry, the Purple Heart and the Navy Commendation Medal. After his wartime service he rose to the rank of Commander in the Naval Reserves. As a sales rep Phil was always one of the top salespeople in the companies for which he worked and a sales manager for three Fortune 500 firms. Later in his business career was also a CEO for four start-up technology firms specializing in the sales and marketing of high-end software products. He is currently CEO of Peconic Bay Consulting in Southampton, New York. In 1999 Phil was selected for the Executive in Residence Program at Long Island University's Business Division and for the next six years taught both undergraduate and graduate courses in business at LIU, Southampton. In 2007 Phil accepted an assignment to teach business topics at the Rhode Island School of Design (RISD) in Providence where he still teaches today. Phil is a columnist for the Southampton Press, a feature writer for magazines, has published two fictional novels, is working on a non-fiction Vietnam book for St. Martin's Press and is President of the Long Island Author's Group. He is a licensed Coast Guard Captain and enjoys boating in and around the east end of Long Island. He lives in Southampton, New York with his partner Laura and son Pierce.

www.ingramcontent.com/pod-product-compliance
Lightning Source LLC
Chambersburg PA
CBHW060643290526
45793CB00001B/369